Encouragement from
BETH
MOORE

with quotations from

Believing God

Breaking Free

Praying God's Word

When Godly People
Do Ungodly Things

May you be
strengthened
with all power,
according to His
glorious might.

Colossians 1:11

We learn to be
victorious only by
surrendering our lives
completely to the Spirit
of God, not by gritting our
teeth and trying harder.

from BREAKING FREE

The testing of
your faith produces
endurance. But
endurance must
do its complete work,
so that you may be
mature and complete,
lacking nothing.

James 1:3–4

Lord, my flesh is so
resistant to what You want
right now that I can hardly
stand it. But don't stop.
Insist upon my best. Insist
upon Your glory. Take me
to the line on this. Don't
let up on me until we've
gone every inch of
the distance.

from PRAYING GOD'S WORD

God is able to make
every grace overflow
to you, so that in every
way, always having
everything you need,
you may excel in
every good work.

2 Corinthians 9:8

I am freed to know
that my God is huge,
and my God is able. So
I know if I don't get
what I asked from Him,
if I'll cooperate, I'll get
something bigger.
I'll know that a greater
yes is in progress.

from BELIEVING GOD

Lord, Your faithful
love reaches to heaven,
Your faithfulness
to the skies. Your
righteousness is like
the highest mountain;
Your judgments,
like the deepest sea.

Psalm 36:5–6

Ask for His love over
and over for the rest of
your days, till your voice is
hoarse, and with shriveled
hand you point to your
own aged heart and with
one dying word, whisper,
"More."

from WHEN GODLY PEOPLE DO UNGODLY THINGS

The Lord is my
strength and my shield;
my heart trusts in Him,
and I am helped.
Therefore my heart
rejoices, and I praise
Him with my song.

Psalm 28:7

Only God can put the pieces of our heart back together again, close up all the wounds, and bind them with a porous bandage that protects from infection, yet keeps the heart free to inhale and exhale love.

from BREAKING FREE

I am the good
shepherd. I know
My own sheep,
and they know Me,
as the Father knows Me,
and I know the Father.
I lay down My life
for the sheep.

John 10:14–15

No one is more pleasurable
to be around than a person
who has had her cup filled
by the Lord Jesus Christ.
He is the only one who is
never overwhelmed by the
depth and length
of our need.

These are written
so that you may believe
Jesus is the Messiah,
the Son of God, and
by believing you may
have life in His name.

John 20:31

Nothing on earth
compares to the strength
God is willing to interject
into lives caught in the act
of believing.

from BELIEVING GOD

It is I who
sweep away your
transgressions
for My own sake
and remember your
sins no more.

Isaiah 43:25

If the Bible is about anything at all, it is about God having mercy on the pitiful plight of men, forgiving their sins, and restoring their lives.

from WHEN GODLY PEOPLE DO UNGODLY THINGS

Jesus said to her,
"Didn't I tell you
that if you believed
you would see the
glory of God?"

John 11:40

Every time we suffer
loss, we encounter an
opportunity for the loss
to bring gain for Jesus' sake
by allowing His life to be
revealed in us.

Do people fall
and not get up again?
If they turn away,
do they not return?

Jeremiah 8:4

If you fall, don't listen to the accusations and jeers of the evil one. Get back up and walk with God again. How many times? Until you're free.

Blessed be the God and
Father of our Lord Jesus
Christ, who has blessed us
with every spiritual blessing
in the heavens, in Christ.

Ephesians 1:3

Blessing is bowing down to receive the expressions of divine favor that in the inner recesses of the human heart and mind make life worth the bother.

from BELIEVING GOD

They conquered him
by the blood of the Lamb
and by the word of their
testimony, for they did
not love their lives in
the face of death.

Revelation 12:11

The more we understand
what the covering of
Christ's blood means, the
more we overcome a foe
that is otherwise far too
strong for us.

from WHEN GODLY PEOPLE DO UNGODLY THINGS

People cry out because
of severe oppression;
they shout for help
from the arm of
the mighty.

Job 35:9

Victory always begins with a cry for help. When we come to the end of ourselves and cry out for help, amazing things happen.

He has sent
Me to heal the
brokenhearted,
to proclaim liberty
to the captives,
and freedom to
the prisoners.

Isaiah 61:1

God wants to bring us
healing, but more than
anything, He wants us
to know our Healer.
Yes, He wants to give us
resurrection life, but more
than that, He wants us to
know the Resurrection
and the Life.

from PRAYING GOD'S WORD

Return to your
fortress, you prisoners
who have hope; today
I declare that I will
restore double to you.

Zechariah 9:12

God's specialty is raising
dead things to life and
making impossible
things possible.

from BELIEVING GOD

We are in the true
One—that is, in His
Son Jesus Christ.
He is the true God
and eternal life.

1 John 5:20

Satan cannot possessively lay hold of us, keep us in a grip, or touch us in a way that will utterly destroy us. We may *feel* destroyed, but we are not.

from WHEN GODLY PEOPLE DO UNGODLY THINGS

As for me,
I will look to the
Lord; I will wait
for the God of
my salvation.

Micah 7:7

Although we need to
be saved from eternal
separation from God only
once, Christ continues His
saving work in us for the
rest of our lives.

from BREAKING FREE

When pride comes,
disgrace follows,
but with humility
comes wisdom.

Proverbs 11:2

The most effective means
the enemy has to keep us
from being full of the
Spirit is to keep us full of
ourselves.

The Lord is a refuge
for the oppressed,
a refuge in times
of trouble.

Psalm 9:9

Our Promised Lands
are characterized by the
presence of victory, not
the absence of opposition.

from BELIEVING GOD

Be very diligent to
love the Lord your
God for your own
well-being.

Joshua 23:11

A head full of biblical
information without a
heart passionately in love
with Christ is terribly
dangerous, a stronghold ·
waiting to happen.

from WHEN GODLY PEOPLE DO UNGODLY THINGS

I will rebuild its
ruins and will set
it up again, so that
those who are left of
mankind may seek
the Lord.

Acts 15:16–17

Christ was a carpenter by trade. Nothing has ever been allowed to crumble in a Christian's life or heritage that God can't reconstruct and use.

Jesus said,
"With men it is
impossible, but not
with God, because
all things are possible
with God."

Mark 10:27

May God remind us daily
that we are loved and
empowered by the One
who brought the universe
into existence with the
mere sound of His voice.
Nothing is impossible
for Him.

from PRAYING GOD'S WORD

He said to me, "I will make you fruitful and numerous; I will make many nations come from you, and I will give this land as an eternal possession to your descendants to come."

Genesis 48:4

The enemy is standing on your God-given ground daring you to take possession of it. Are you going to let him have it? Or are you going to claim your inheritance? Possession is the law of the Promised Land. Red Rover, go over.

from BELIEVING GOD

For we do not
have a high priest who is
unable to sympathize with
our weaknesses, but One
who has been tested in
every way as we are,
yet without sin.

Hebrews 4:15

When God tests His
children, His purpose is
to prove godly character,
or perhaps the lack thereof.
But if testing exposes a
lack, God's chief desire is
to enlist our cooperation
and provide what
is lacking.

from WHEN GODLY PEOPLE DO UNGODLY THINGS

Godliness is beneficial
in every way, since it
holds promise for the
present life and also
for the life to come.

1 Timothy 4:8

The wonders God wants
to do in all our tomorrows
are prepared for in
our todays.

from BREAKING FREE

We have come to
know and to believe
the love that God has
for us. God is love, and
the one who remains in
love remains in God,
and God remains
in him.

1 John 4:16

If God always delivered us instantly, we would see His greatness once, but we would soon forget. On the other hand, if He teaches us victory in Christ day by day, we live in the constant awareness of His greatness and sufficiency.

from PRAYING GOD'S WORD

The fear of
the Lord is pure,
enduring forever;
the ordinances of
the Lord are reliable
and altogether
righteous.

Psalm 19:9

Most of us believe
God is who He says He is,
but we are less quick to
believe He can do what He
says He can do. Ironically,
however, God can do
what He says He can do
precisely because He is
who He says He is.

from BELIEVING GOD

They will fight
because the Lord is
with them, and they
will put horsemen
to shame.

Zechariah 10:5

All the hosts of heaven
are rooting for you, and all
the unholy hosts of hell are
jeering at you. Win a
big one for the team,
won't you?

from WHEN GODLY PEOPLE DO UNGODLY THINGS

If only you had
paid attention to
My commands.
Then your peace
would have been
like a river, and your
righteousness like the
waves of the sea.

Isaiah 48:18

God's Word does not
say we'll have peace like a
pond. To have peace like a
river is to have security and
tranquility even while
meeting many bumps
and unexpected turns
on life's journey.

from BREAKING FREE

Sown in dishonor,
raised in glory;
sown in weakness,
raised in power.

1 Corinthians 15:43

God's strength is
tailor-made for weakness.
We are never stronger
than when we admit we
are weak.

The vision is yet for the appointed time; it testifies about the end and will not lie. Though it delays, wait for it, since it will certainly come and not be late.

Habakkuk 2:3

I am utterly convinced that any *no* an earnestly seeking child of God receives from the Throne is for the sake of a greater *yes,* whether realized on earth or in heaven.

Large crowds would
come together to hear
Him and to be healed of
their sicknesses. Yet He
often withdrew to deserted
places and prayed.

Luke 5:15–16

Love is the stuff of intimacy. We can never learn intimacy in even the most anointed corporate worship. We discover divine love in the inexplicable freedom of solitary confinement with God.

from WHEN GODLY PEOPLE DO UNGODLY THINGS

His master said
to him, "Well done,
good and faithful slave!
You were faithful over
a few things; I will put you
in charge of many things.
Share your master's joy!"

Matthew 25:21

Christ wants us to share
His happiness, to live
happily ever after. Until
then, He gives us a sudden
splash of happiness here
and there so we can wet
our toes in what we'll
be swimming in for all
of eternity!

from BREAKING FREE

The Spirit lifted
me up and brought
me to the inner
court, and the glory
of the Lord filled
the temple.

Ezekiel 43:5

I know from experience
that so much of the shame
we experience is wrapped
up in the secret. But once
we expose the secret places
of our lives to the light of
God's Word, we're on our
way to freedom.

from PRAYING GOD'S WORD

The Lord is certain
to bless you in the land
the Lord your God is
giving you to possess as an
inheritance—if only you
obey the Lord your God.

Deuteronomy 15:4–5

Obedience to God in
a difficult situation will
ultimately bear fruit, even
though it looks like
it might immediately
cause hardship.

from BELIEVING GOD

Do not be
conformed to this age,
but be transformed by the
renewing of your mind, so
that you may discern what
is the good, pleasing, and
perfect will of God.

Romans 12:2

We have a responsibility
to one another, which
means we have a
responsibility to become
the kinds of people who
can help one another
responsibly.

from WHEN GODLY PEOPLE DO UNGODLY THINGS

Let us be glad, rejoice,
and give Him glory,
because the marriage
of the Lamb has come,
and His wife has
prepared herself.

Revelation 19:7

We cannot make ourselves
ready to meet Christ the
moment we see Him any
more than a woman can be
prepared to meet her
groom at the altar with
three minutes' notice.
I don't want to be caught
with spiritual curlers in
my hair!

from BREAKING FREE

Restore the joy
of Your salvation
to me, and give me
a willing spirit.

Psalm 51:12

Obedience to God is not some diet we suddenly blow. It is something to which we recommit every single day, no matter how we blew it the day before.

from PRAYING GOD'S WORD

Because he is
lovingly devoted to Me,
I will deliver him;
I will exalt him, because
he knows My name.

Psalm 91:14

Satan has no right to exercise authority over us, but he hopes we're too ignorant regarding Scripture to know it. Knowing and claiming God's Word when attacked blows the head off enemy forces.

from BELIEVING GOD

I don't say this out of need,
for I have learned to be
content in whatever
circumstances I am.

Philippians 4:11

The grass is never greener
on the other side of the
fence. It's nothing but
artificial coloring.

The Lord your God
is testing you to know
whether you love the
Lord your God with
all your heart and
all your soul.

Deuteronomy 13:3

God does not take our
spiritual temperature under
the tongue by the words we
say, nor in our ear by the
impressive teachings we
hear, nor under our arms
by the service we perform.
God takes our spiritual
temperature straight from
the heart.

from BREAKING FREE

Do not judge, and
you will not be judged.
Do not condemn, and you
will not be condemned.
Forgive, and you will
be forgiven.

Luke 6:37

We never look more
like Christ than when
we forgive. And since that's
God's goal, we're destined
to have plenty of
opportunities!

I delight to do
Your will, my God;
Your instruction
resides within me.

Psalm 40:8

Nothing is a greater threat
to the enemy than a
believer with the Word
of God living and active
upon her tongue, readily
applied to any situation.

from BELIEVING GOD

Throw off all the
transgressions you have
committed, and make
yourselves a new heart
and a new spirit.

Ezekiel 18:31

Very likely, wherever
you are on your road
to restoration, you are
somewhere between having
a thousand feelings and
having none at all. That's
okay. All you need to get
started is to know you
need to get started.

from WHEN GODLY PEOPLE DO UNGODLY THINGS

If anyone serves Me,
he must follow Me.
Where I am, there
My servant also will be.
If anyone serves Me,
the Father will
honor him.

John 12:26

Satan tries to draw us away from God's authority by making us think we can be our own producer and director. But God did not design us to boss ourselves. He formed our psyches to require authority so we'd live in the safety of His careful rule.

from BREAKING FREE

You Yourself
have recorded my
wanderings. Put my
tears in Your bottle.
Are they not in
Your records?

Psalm 56:8

God anguishes over our
suffering, yet He waits
until the tears that have
fallen on dry ground or
upon the shoulders of
others equally frail are
poured instead before
His throne.

Remind them
of these things,
charging them
before God not
to fight about
words.

2 Timothy 2:14

Frivolous arguments can
dilute spiritual truths into
human logic. We are not
called to debate faith but
to do it, to be nouns
turned into verbs.
Presently. Actively.

from BELIEVING GOD

You must take
up the full armor
of God, so that
you may be able
to resist in
the evil day.

Ephesians 6:13

The first piece of
armor to put back on
is the breastplate of
righteousness. That way,
your injured heart will be
protected by your *doing*
what is right until you *feel*
what is right.

from WHEN GODLY PEOPLE DO UNGODLY THINGS

He has sent Me
for His glory against
the nations who are
plundering you, for
anyone who touches
you touches the pupil
of His eye.

Zechariah 2:8

I've slowly come to trust
God's sovereignty enough
to believe that anyone I
must obey on this earth
had better be careful with
me, or they have God to
answer to!

from BREAKING FREE

A thief comes
only to steal and to
kill and to destroy.
I have come that
they may have life
and have it in
abundance.

John 10:10

Physical existence is
not what Christ died to
bring us. He came that we
might have life and have
it more abundantly. As
impossible as this truth
may seem, God can
restore abundant life.

from PRAYING GOD'S WORD

You love Him,
though you have not
seen Him. And though
not seeing Him now,
you believe in Him and
rejoice with inexpressible
and glorious joy.

1 Peter 1:8

Stop looking at others as
being more spiritual than
you and just starting
believing God! He's not
looking for spiritual giants.
God is looking for
believers who *believe*
for a change.

from BELIEVING GOD

The end of
a matter is better
than its beginning;
a patient spirit is
better than a
proud spirit.

Ecclesiastes 7:8

Every time God steps
on your pride and it yells,
"Ouch!" ask Him to
go ahead and stomp on
it until He kills the
wicked thing.

from WHEN GODLY PEOPLE DO UNGODLY THINGS

Knowing the time,
it is already the hour
for you to wake up
from sleep, for now
our salvation is
nearer than when
we first believed.

Romans 13:11

We were created to give
Christ's invisible character
a glimpse of visibility.
If we grasp the eternal
implications of such a
destiny, we would want to
do anything possible to
make sure all hindrances
are removed.

from BREAKING FREE

Then they may
come to their senses
and escape the Devil's
trap, having been
captured by him
to do his will.

2 Timothy 2:26

When we are challenged to repent of cherished sin, all God is waiting for us to do is invite Him to change our hearts and bring about the supernatural work of true repentance.

from PRAYING GOD'S WORD

I am able
to do all things
through Him who
strengthens me.

Philippians 4:13

We *can* do all things
through Christ who
strengthens us,
but frankly we *won't* if
we're too afraid to try.

In Him we have
redemption through
His blood, the forgiveness
of our trespasses, according
to the riches of His grace
that He lavished on us
with all wisdom and
understanding.

Ephesians 1:7–8

The same God who
knew in advance that you
would become one of His
children also knew in
advance that you'd be
susceptible to fall for a
deceptive scheme of the
evil one. Still, He says
you were adopted
with pleasure.

from WHEN GODLY PEOPLE DO UNGODLY THINGS

The Lord is near all
who call out to Him,
all who call out to Him
with integrity. He fulfills
the desires of those who
fear Him; He hears
their cry for help
and saves them.

Psalm 145:18–19

Hearts that are not
surrendered to God can
seldom be trusted. Until
we surrender our hopes
and dreams to Christ,
we really have very little
way of knowing what
would fulfill us.

from BREAKING FREE

Your love has delivered
me from the Pit of
destruction, for You
have thrown all my sins
behind Your back.

Isaiah 38:17

Our hearts are not healthy
until they have been
satisfied by the only
completely healthy
love that exists:
the love of God.

from PRAYING GOD'S WORD

In Your presence is
abundant joy; in Your
right hand are eternal
pleasures.

Psalm 16:11

No sin, no matter how
momentarily pleasurable,
comforting, or habitual, is
worth missing what God
has for us.

My Father is
glorified by this:
that you produce
much fruit and
prove to be My
disciples.

John 15:8

We will never cease to
be God's children,
but when we cease
learning and being
teachable, we are no
longer disciples.

from WHEN GODLY PEOPLE DO UNGODLY THINGS

Now may the God
of hope fill you with
all joy and peace in
believing, so that you
may overflow with
hope by the power
of the Holy Spirit.

Romans 15:13

A crucial part of fleshing
out our liberation in Christ
means allowing Him to fill
the empty places in our
lives. I'm not talking about
a life full of activities.
I'm talking about a soul
full of Jesus.

from BREAKING FREE

Lord, You have
heard the desire of
the humble; You will
strengthen their
hearts. You will
listen carefully.

Psalm 10:17

I am convinced that God
would rather hear our
honest pleas for more of
what we lack than a host
of pious platitudes from
an unbelieving heart.

I have set before
you life and death,
blessing and curse.
Choose life so that
you and your
descendants
may live.

Deuteronomy 30:19

We know we're coming
full circle with God when
we stand at a very similar
crossroad where we made
such a mess of life before,
but this time we take a
different road.

from BELIEVING GOD

Let us draw near
with a true heart in
full assurance of faith,
our hearts sprinkled
clean from an evil
conscience and our
bodies washed
in pure water.

Hebrews 10:22

You and I realize that the blood Christ shed on the cross is the means of remission for our sins. It is also the means for the complete cleansing of the consciences of those who already know Christ.

from WHEN GODLY PEOPLE DO UNGODLY THINGS

How happy is
the man who has
put his trust in the
Lord and has not
turned to the proud
or to those who
run after lies!

Psalm 40:4

Trusting an invisible God doesn't come naturally for any believer. A trust relationship grows only by stepping out in faith and making the choice to trust. The ability to believe God develops most often through pure experience.

from BREAKING FREE

No weapon formed against
you will succeed, and you
will refute any accusation
raised against you in court.
This is the heritage of the
Lord's servants, and their
righteousness is from Me.

Isaiah 54:17

Know the truth so
thoroughly and respond
to conviction so readily
that when accusations
come, you can resist the
devil, no matter whose
voice grants him volume.

You do not have
to fight this battle.
Position yourselves,
stand still, and see
the salvation of
the Lord.

2 Chronicles 20:17

Fighting the good fight
of faith takes energy!
So do self-pity, anger,
unforgiveness, and
self-loathing. Each of
us must decide where
we're going to put our
energy when the battle
grows fierce.

from BELIEVING GOD

Much more then,
since we have now
been declared
righteous by His
blood, we will be
saved through
Him from
wrath.

Romans 5:9

Once we repent of our sins, Christ not only serves as our counselor and attorney; He also files the most glorious legal brief in the universe. He declares that all punishment and payment of fines for our crimes have been met.

from WHEN GODLY PEOPLE DO UNGODLY THINGS

Some of you
will rebuild the
ancient ruins; you will
restore the foundations
laid long ago; you will
be called the repairer
of broken walls, the
restorer of streets
where people live.

Isaiah 58:12

The Ancient of Days is
waiting to build a solid
foundation that your
descendants can live on
for years to come if they
choose. He's not asking us
to rebuild ancient ruins
by ourselves. He's simply
asking us to be one of
the tools He uses.

from BREAKING FREE

Put on heartfelt
compassion, kindness,
humility, gentleness, and
patience, accepting one
another and forgiving one
another if anyone has a
complaint against another.

Colossians 3:12–13

Praying about a person
we need to forgive is the
means by which we tip the
pitcher heavenward and
slowly begin to pour our
negative feelings and
frustrations out to God.

from PRAYING GOD'S WORD

She weeps
aloud during
the night,
with tears on
her cheeks.

Lamentations 1:2

I don't know about you,
but I tend to be a lot
gutsier in my vocalized
prayers, because hearing
them with my own ears
often ignites my heart
and mind all the more.

from BELIEVING GOD

The Lord will
grant you a blessing
on your storehouses
and on everything
you do; He will bless
you in the land the
Lord your God
is giving you.

Deuteronomy 28:8

When I'm feeling down
or a little like a brat,
I often sense God speaking
to my heart, saying,
"Name 'em, child."
He means start naming a
mere twenty or thirty of
the thousands of ways He's
shown His goodness to me.

from WHEN GODLY PEOPLE DO UNGODLY THINGS

Yes, Lord,
we wait for You
in the path of
Your judgments.
Our desire is for
Your name and
renown.

Isaiah 26:8

Any time we glorify God, we are displays of His splendor. But right now I want to paint a portrait of a life that truly withholds nothing from God, a life through which God does something only He can do.

from BREAKING FREE

What more could I
have done for My vineyard
than I did? Why, when I
expected a yield of good
grapes, did it yield
worthless grapes?

Isaiah 5:4

What heartbreak we must bring to the God when we continue to disbelieve His love. What more could He have said? What more could He have done?

All mankind has
seen it; people have
looked at it from a
distance. Look, God
is exalted beyond our
knowledge; the number
of His years cannot
be counted.

Job 36:25–26

I don't care how intelligent
the deceiver seems or how
well-meaning and sincere
his or her doctrine. If in
our pursuit of greater
knowledge, God seems to
have gotten smaller, we
have been deceived.

from BELIEVING GOD

Take words of repentance
with you and return to the
Lord. Say to Him: "Forgive
all our sin and accept what
is good, so that we may
repay You with praise
from our lips."

Hosea 14:2

After all God has
done for me, if I were to
withhold from the Pharisee
the right to splash in the
river of forgiveness, it
would make me a bigger
one than he.

from WHEN GODLY PEOPLE DO UNGODLY THINGS

Whatever you do,
do it enthusiastically,
as something done for
the Lord and not for men,
knowing that you will
receive the reward of
an inheritance from
the Lord—you serve
the Lord Christ.

Colossians 3:23–24

Whenever the enemy tries to use your physical lineage against you, use your spiritual lineage against him! As a child of God and a joint heir with Christ, refuse the enemy a single inch of the ground you are taking back.

from BREAKING FREE

Be sober! Be on the alert!
Your adversary the Devil is
prowling around like a
roaring lion, looking for
anyone he can devour.

1 Peter 5:8

Satan is an opportunist.
Would he come after
you when you are down?
In a heartbeat. If he
had a heart.

Then you will delight
yourself in the Lord,
and I will make you ride
over the heights of the
land, and let you enjoy
the heritage of your
father Jacob.

Isaiah 58:14

I assure you, God and I have made some memories together. Hard ones. Good ones. Astounding ones. You don't have to know God long to make memories with Him.

from BELIEVING GOD

By obedience
to the truth,
having purified
yourselves for sincere
love of the brothers,
love one another
earnestly from
a pure heart.

1 Peter 1:22

I finally allowed a group of
people to see right through
me. And they love me
anyway. Oh, what joy!
A joy I will no longer allow
the enemy to steal.
Somewhere along the way,
the Cover Girl broke free.
She may not be pretty.
But she's real.

from WHEN GODLY PEOPLE DO UNGODLY THINGS

Let all who
seek You rejoice
and be glad in You;
let those who love
Your salvation
continually say,
"The Lord is great!"

Psalm 40:16

I fear we may have become so legalistic that we've dropped the word *happy* from our religious vocabulary. Allow me to get this off my chest once and for all. Sometimes God just plain makes me happy! Call me immature, but picture me smiling.

from BREAKING FREE

The Lord said to me,
"You have seen correctly,
for I watch over My word
to accomplish it."

Jeremiah 1:12

Give him *time* and *truth*,
and there's nothing God
can't do. You be willing to
provide the sweat and tears,
but know that He's already
provided the blood.

from PRAYING GOD'S WORD

I am certain that
I will see the Lord's
goodness in the land
of the living. Wait for the
Lord; be courageous and
let your heart be strong.
Wait for the Lord.

Psalm 27:13–14.

Sometimes God requires us
to follow a fair amount
of repetition for a
considerable amount of
time until He deems a
season complete. Then all
of a sudden, He seems to
do something profound or
miraculous, and we can't
figure out what changed.

from BELIEVING GOD

Before a word is
on my tongue, You
know all about it, Lord.
You have encircled me;
You have placed Your hand
on me. This extraordinary
knowledge is beyond me.
It is lofty; I am unable
to reach it.

Psalm 139:4–6

I could go to the
furthest reaches of human
vocabulary, studying the
languages of every people
to find who says it best,
and still my efforts would
be frustrated by this divine
affection that exceeds
description.

from WHEN GODLY PEOPLE DO UNGODLY THINGS

Grace has come
from the Lord our God
to preserve a remnant
for us and give us a stake
in His holy place. Even
in our slavery, God has
given us new life and
light to our eyes.

Ezra 9:8

Have you been among
the living dead? The
stone's been rolled away.
Resurrection life awaits
you. Will you continue to
sit in a dark tomb, or will
you walk into the light
of resurrection life?
Lazarus, come forth!

from BREAKING FREE

Wake up, wake up;
put on your strength, Zion!
Put on your beautiful
garments, Jerusalem, the
Holy City! For the
uncircumcised and the
unclean will no longer
enter you. Stand up,
shake the dust off
yourself!

Isaiah 52:1–2

When we approach God in genuine repentance, taking full responsibility for our own sins, our prison doors swing open. But tragically, we could sit in our prison cells for the next five years in torment if we don't stand on God's promises and walk forward in truth.

from PRAYING GOD'S WORD

The idolaters eagerly seek
all these things, and your
heavenly Father knows that
you need them. But seek
first the kingdom of God
and His righteousness, and
all these things will be
provided for you.

Matthew 6:32–33

A big difference exists
between trying to
manipulate God to give
us what we want, and
cooperating with God
so He can give us
what *He* wants.

from BELIEVING GOD

You have put more joy
in my heart than they have
when their grain and new
wine abound. I will both
lie down and sleep in
peace, for You alone, Lord,
make me live in safety.

Psalm 4:7–8

We are saved by Christ alone. And on the day of our complete and perfect redemption, face-to-face with Jesus, we will be safe in the hands of the One to whom we've been sent.

The remnant of Israel
and the survivors of the
house of Jacob will no
longer depend on the
one who struck them,
but they will faithfully
depend on the Lord,
the Holy One
of Israel.

Isaiah 10:20

More than you seek to
defeat the enemy, seek his
foe! More than you seek
victory, seek the Victor!
You'll never be more
beautiful to God than
when He can look down
and see you hanging on to
Him for dear life!

from BREAKING FREE

The Lord commanded
me to teach you statutes
and ordinances for you to
follow in the land you are
about to cross into and
possess. Be extremely
careful for your
own good.

Deuteronomy 4:14–15

For folks like me
and every other overcomer
I have known personally,
there's not a lot of gray
when it comes to walking
with Christ. I've learned the
hard way what can happen
when you wander too close
to a hole. You can fall in.

I have not departed
from the commands of
His lips; I have treasured
the words of His mouth
more than my daily food.

Job 23:12

I am a woman with a
human nature heavily given
to sin, but I have not lived
out of that powerful old
nature in a long time.
We are making it, God
and I, one day at a time.

from BELIEVING GOD

While the son was still a long way off, his father saw him and was filled with compassion. He ran, threw his arms around his neck, and kissed him.

Luke 15:20

Your healing will come
in your very own Abba's
tight and passionate
embrace. Let Him hold
you so close that you can
hear His heart pounding
from having run to you.

from WHEN GODLY PEOPLE DO UNGODLY THINGS

We demolish arguments
and every high-minded
thing that is raised up
against the knowledge
of God, taking every
thought captive to the
obedience of Christ.

2 Corinthians 10:4–5

You and I have been
controlled and held
prisoner by destructive,
negative, and misleading
thoughts for too long.
Through the power of the
Holy Spirit, we can take
our thoughts prisoner
instead.

from BREAKING FREE

God is not a man
who lies, or a son of
man who changes His
mind. Does He speak
and not act, or promise
and not fulfill?

Numbers 23:19

God's faithfulness cannot
be fathomed by comparing
Him to the noblest of
men. God is not a man.
He does not simply resist
ignoble tendencies. He
lacks them altogether.

from PRAYING GOD'S WORD